Conquering the Baby Bar: Your Comprehensive Guide to the First-Year Law Students' Examination

By Lenora S. Lapesarde

Printed in the United States of America

First Printing, 2016

Legal Eagle Press
ISBN-13: 978-0692643709
ISBN-10: 0692643702

Llapesarde@Gmail.com

For Milan Lapesarde, I love you more than anything. Jewel and Joaquina Lapesarde who have supported me through this Law School journey. Thank you mom and dad.

And for the Peoples College of Law. It was founded on the principles of commitment to social justice and change and have unwaveringly lived this mission.

TABLE OF CONTENTS

INTRODUCTION

And so it begins. The first day of law school is when you start to take steps toward your next goal; doing well on your exams and passing the FYLSX. During this process you will develop the tools to succeed by following the advice of your professors, using the tactics described in this book, and keeping a consistent study schedule.

There's no substitute for hard work but there are ways to use your time that will let you learn and retain lots of information in less time. Read on to find out how to develop a study strategy that has been created for the first year of law school and the FYLSX.

Law school is hard. You learn to use logic and law in order to be a reliable consultant for people in need of legal advice. You are in charge of analyzing problems and advising them with ethical, correct guidance. To do this accurately a lawyer has to think in terms of the relationships between the facts presented by the parties, applicable laws, and how to present the best case. That's one of the main reasons why a legal education is so rigorous. You are going to be held to a high standard by professional committees, clients, and judges. It's time to hold YOURSELF to these standards today.

This doesn't mean that you will chew your pencils down to stubs while studying ten hours a day. Your goal is to study effectively so you don't have to spend your life in the library. Good grades aren't based on total hours of study; the grades are based on your analysis and understanding on test day. Putting in seventy hours a week isn't sustainable. So step one is learning how to study smart.

One goal is to shorten study hours by storing information in your long term memory. A lot of students put in countless hours of study only to discover months later that they've forgotten much of the information.

It's a waste of valuable time if you have to end up re-learning topics. That leads to disappointment and less than stellar grades. The key to counteracting that issue is to learn storage techniques so you won't have to review the same material over and over again just to get some of it in your permanent memory bank.

In California there is another way to become a lawyer besides the traditional ABA method. Non ABA accredited schools are a low cost option for students. One reason why this route is so attractive is because those of us who wish to work serving community interests, social justice, or civil rights can graduate with limited debt and go directly into our chosen discipline without the stress of paying back exorbitant student loans. The legal road is littered with attorneys who began school with a desire to help others but practical matters forced them to abandon that principle and join the legion of lawyers who boast lofty credentials yet have to wage battle for middling jobs.

The US. News and World Report revealed that newly graduating lawyers are starting their careers off with a debt load that averages an astounding 134,000 dollars! In their 2008 study they reported that 36.2% of Law (LLB or JD) students had six figure debt loads. Non ABA students can graduate with no debt.

Why doesn't everyone just do this? Well, students who choose to attend a non ABA school face an extra hurdle. So, what's the catch? The catch is that you have to pass an exam called the FYLSX, also known as the Baby Bar, to move onto your second year of study.

One of the struggles facing the student who forgoes an ABA education is navigating the traditional law school method of learning, the "how to think", with the non-traditional burden that requires that 1L's become "Bar Perfect" in three subjects.

"Bar Perfect" goes beyond the basic familiarity that traditional students have and means that you have to be prepared to take the Bar in those three areas at the end of the first year. No wonder there is such a high fail rate! It's a lot to ask of someone who just completed 1L.

WHAT'S THE DEAL WITH THE FYLSX?

The caveat to attending non accredited schools or reading the law under an apprenticeship is the requirement that those who do so must pass an exam known as the First Year Law Student Exam (FYLSX) colloquially known as the "Baby Bar." This test is administered by the California Bar Association twice a year. The exam has an 80% fail rate. This book is intended to get you into the 20% who pass each term.

California also has the nation's toughest Bar exam, the last term only 48% of the takers passed. Those statistics aren't presented to frighten you. Rather, they are here to motivate you. Determination and a solid academic plan will produce successful results. If you develop proper study habits now then the Bar shouldn't be much trouble.

The FYLSX is a major hurdle for many people attending a non ABA school and there isn't a lot of information on how to pass out there. It took some trial and error before figuring out what a successful academic plan looked like. But it worked. I passed the FYLSX on my first attempt and one of my essays was published as a model answer for by the State Bar for the June 2014 torts portion. My first fail in law school was also for a torts essay. Our professor was not one for low expectations and she brought out the best in all of us which required tough love. Needless to say torts was a high priority after that first zero.

I didn't have a clue how to study productively when law school began. I figured that my usual laissez faire attitude that sailed me through my prior eduction would keep working. Once the reading and assignments started coming in I was unprepared for the onslaught and worried that test day would arrive before I was ready.

I didn't take any of the commercial programs, study groups, and did not use any tutors. The plan that worked for me and my budget entailed buying a variety of books on each subject, reading, outlining, and using memory techniques to retain all the new information.

It also required balancing the traditional method of learning and the full in depth understanding of torts, contracts, and criminal law that the FYLSX requires. It took some trial and error to develop a plan that was going to get all the right information stored but if you get on it early and stay disciplined you can do it.

You may already be familiar with the format of the FYLSX, but let's go over it in case you are a new student or just to fill in any blanks. The First Year Law Student Exam is a standardized full day test that is administered and proctored by the California State Bar (Cal Bar). If you sat for the LSAT then you have a pretty good idea of the rigors involved in taking a Cal Bar test.

They maintain strict security and only a few items such as pencils, highlighters, an admittance ticket, and identification are allowed into the testing room. During the essay portion of the test you may use a laptop and then remove it to the antechamber after that portion of the exam has ended. If you require ADA accommodations then those must be arranged in advance with the Bar. If you have any sort of ability issue you should definitely look into this to maximize your chances of success.

Before the test there are hundreds of test takers milling bout as well as dozens of proctors and security. It's the cattle call that will define many peoples futures so there is certainly an air of drama and nerves. There is emotion and tension and the atmosphere is electric. Hundreds of people are feeling the same anticipation that will envelope you. That shouldn't hold you back or intimidate you. Think of it as fuel for the race ahead and just go for it. You're going to be nervous too, but there are some tips to get you through that in a later chapter.

The exam is given in Pasadena and San Francisco in June and October. There are usually between 600-800 applicants each go round. The structure of the exam is broken into two parts. First up is a four hour period consisting of four essays. They will test you on Torts, Contracts, and Criminal law with an additional essay that duplicates one of those three topics.

The moment that you flip the page on the booklet containing these essays is a scary moment, but to pass you have to be brave and take a breath, then... jump. Jump right into the first pattern and don't stop thinking, writing, or analyzing for one single second of those four hours. When you take stretch breaks every 15-20 minutes spend that time thinking about what you will write next.

The second session comes after a one hour lunch break. Typically there is less "lunching" and "breaking" than there is talking about what you did or didn't do wrong. Even if you felt that you bombed, don't harp on the negative or even worse... walk away from the first half expecting that you failed the essays. Many people overestimate their essays and fail; many people seriously devalue their efforts in the first half and basically give up before they have had the chance to get to the second part.

The test is a war and there are two battles to be fought, do not let the first one interfere with the second. During the break eat something or have a coffee. Drink some water and have a bathroom break. Don't forget your physical body. You need your brain to have adequate glucose, a quiet bladder, and sound fingers to do your best work.

The second session is a one hundred question multiple-choice section. You are given 3 hours to complete this section. Easy peasy, right? Yeah, no. It's not, but it's very doable and takes preparation. By the time you sit down to take this test you should have hundreds, if not thousands, of practice questions under your belt. There are a finite number of ways any issue can be presented and if you are familiar with them you can recognize the issue even with the specific names and scenarios changed.

Maybe you are a 0L looking for a leg up, a 1L in the thick of it, or you could be a repeater looking for a fresh take. The advice is the same. Identifying your learning type is first step so that you don't waste time implementing strategies that aren't well suited to your learning style. Making a study plan is the next move, this will keep you focused on your goal and let you track how much time you are investing in each area. We will then move on and cover how to get cheap material to study with and different methods to prepare for the test.

This examination will test your will, knowledge, and mental stamina. Passive reading and tapping away on a keyboard isn't sufficient because law school requires you to develop active processing and analysis skills. You really need to get your hands dirty with a test of this magnitude and prepare all of these attributes well in advance.

Make outlines, flowcharts, write out the definitions repeatedly until everything becomes second nature. Pick up a newspaper and analyze the crimes, the contracts, the accidents that you read about and figure out what laws apply to the stories.

CHAPTER 1: BECOMING A 20 PERCENTER: PASSING A TEST THAT HAS AN 80% FAIL RATE

"You must train harder than the enemy who is trying to kill you. You will get all the rest you need in the grave." — *Leon Degrelle*

Never let go of your focus. The exams that you have during law school are your enemies and you are a general preparing to do battle. Don't lull yourself into the false comfort of your books; strive every day to learn something new or broaden your understanding of an already familiar concept. Everyone who has been through law school says that the first year is the hardest. They aren't lying.

It's the hardest because you are literally reprogramming your entire way of thinking. Have you ever run into someone and thought after a moment, "That's a lawyer."? There's a particular affect that many attorneys have that is instantly recognizable to anyone with experience with lawyers. It's because of the training. The brain gets wired to think in a rational manner and become less outwardly emotional because you will be able to argue both sides of any issue, irregardless of your actual personal feelings.

It would be wonderful if we could learn the law by watching Law and Order reruns and reading John Grisham novels. Unfortunately, that's not the case and the exam is going to require every ounce of focus that you can muster. Studying for law school is training for an important part of your life- your career. Although the law is an absorbing, wonderful vocation it has quite a bit of language and theory that needs to be learned in a consistent fashion in order to become successful. You will be exhausted many times over before you graduate and then another few months of work is still left to take and pass the Bar. After that's all done then you can take a well deserved vacation and relax.

Simply learning the black letter definitions isn't enough. You are going to study a strange new way of organizing your writing- Its called **IRAC** and it stands for *Issue, Rule, Analysis, Conclusion*. Start learning to format your writing like this early in the year because all of your essays, including Bar essays, must be written in IRAC.

Law school is about teaching you how to think, which is why the preferred method of legal study is based on the Socratic Method. The teacher poses questions and issues are explored as a class. Learning the facts while also learning the analysis takes some juggling and the FYLSX requirement means that you don't have much time to waste.

ABA students don't have to worry about the Bar for years. You've got 9 months to get Bar perfect in three subjects. How are you supposed to do that? Well, practice active thinking while you study. Engage your entire brain in the process by thinking about why a case is the way it is. Do practice questions deliberately so that you understand why the answer is correct and then write out the correct answer so that it sticks in your mind. There's a lot of bulk material that you have to memorize as well so the study process is about balancing these two requirements.

The first few weeks of any law course is going to seem like a whole new language. This is true whether you are studying Torts, Contracts, Evidence, or the Constitution. It's a whole new world and it's easy to become overwhelmed. The best thing to do the first few weeks of any class is to learn as if you were dropped in a foreign land and learning a new tongue. Read, listen, and absorb and don't get intimidated by the arcane language and new use of terms. You will never view the words "reasonable", "intent", "negligent", or many other words with the same lens again.

When you first begin classes you should hold off writing essays or practicing multi-choice questions. Immerse yourself in the books and cases, and of course pay very close attention to your professors during class. They will guide you through this process and are generally happy to answer well considered questions. Passing down knowledge is a major part of the human experience, so always treat them with the utmost respect and deference; they are doing a great service by sharing their expertise. Your professors, administrators, and in-school support staff all want you to succeed.

A well stocked personal library is an asset. You are going to have spare time during the first few weeks some time so buy as many as you can afford. There is a later chapter on how to buy reasonably priced books. Even if a book seems like it's over your head or is on an advanced topic you should buy it anyways and stick it on the shelf for later. You are going to need it later.

After the initial immersion you that are going to begin harder work. Week two and three is when you are going to stretch those new legal muscles. Don't be afraid to answer ten multi-choice questions and get all ten wrong. You're going to need to learn by trial and error and at first it's more error than not.

Lots of people rush out of the gate in law school and throw themselves to the wolves, I mean the books, and burn out before they reach the end of the year. This year is going to be taxing enough without running blindly into the fray. Make your game plan and stick to it because it won't do any good to study sixty hours a week for the first two months and six hours a week as the semester winds down.

There's a 10% rule in running that states that you should not increase your speed by more than 10% per week as you grow in ability. This is good advice not only for running but for learning as well. If you start with two hours a day of study in just five weeks you will be up to three hours and twenty minutes.

The end of the semester is when you have absorbed enough of the language and ideas to push yourself harder and really start delving into the theories of the topic that you are working on. Essay writing is not first week or second week material. Definitions definitely are. Keep a steady pace throughout the semester, slowly ramping up the hours and types of study as you become more familiar with the definitions, elements, and theory of the law.

The other side of that coin is that you will never feel 100% ready to start doing essays but you're going to have to do them anyway. A month or two into law school is when you should start practicing them on your own. Begin too soon and you will just confuse yourself, too late and you won't have time to get enough experience.

WHY DO 80% OF FYLSX THE APPLICANTS FAIL

The total law school failure rate depends on many different variables; study habits, core legal knowledge, writing speed, ability, and quality of previous education are just a few. The GPA and LSAT requirements of major law schools are in place to weed out people who lack the inherent ability to get through law school. They aren't always right; in fact, many suitable applicants are denied the law school advantage because of biased factors.

It's a fact that many people are denied a legal education because of socio-economic reasons, test scores, or perceived ability. Nationally the first year dropout rate for top level schools is fairly high, averaging at around 20%. This means that the intellectual criteria that major schools base their selections on aren't always on the money. The real determination on who will succeed is based on other attributes such as ambition, mental stamina, self-discipline, and time management.

Think of law students as a herd of gazelles; sharp, smart, lithe, and eager. Then consider the lions you will encounter before becoming a lawyer: GPA stats, LSAT scores, law school exams, external life situations, the FYLSX, and the State Bar. These are all constructs that you can face and then overcome in your way of becoming a lawyer if you adequately prepare.

You are reading this because you don't want to be the slow gazelle and that alone gives you an advantage. Savor your ambition and use it to propel yourself into your legal career. Successful people put in a lot of hard work to reach their goals. There's no such thing as an ambivalent astronaut or a lackadaisical C.E.O because ambitious people know that anything worth doing is worth doing well.

Being a self-learned person who can utilize mental resources and skills to get through the challenges of life is a very powerful thing. Law is one of the few great professions that still recognize an autodidactic path in some capacity. Many other professions have lost this fine art. As a student in a non ABA school the ability to sit down and spend time self-educating is what will make the difference between a pass or a fail. There simply aren't enough class hours in school to give you all of the knowledge that you will need.

On the other hand, it's important to come into law school understanding that you don't really know the law at all. Some students who are great at self education shoot themselves in the foot because they are well read and "know the law." Some students who have been activists or worked in a legal capacity don't study as much because they feel well versed in the field. Law school isn't about concrete knowledge, it's about learning how to think. Come in with an open mind and let your professors and books fill your head up.

CHAPTER 2: FIGURING OUT HOW YOU LEARN BEST

First off, how do you learn best? The answer to that question will help you create study materials tailored to your strengths. If this is your first time encountering this question or you haven't considered it in a while take some time to really think about it. All the practice lectures, exam essays, and MBE questions in the world won't help you pass if you cannot make a solid study plan that melds your own personal learning strengths with the particulars of the test. The FYLSX measures your legal knowledge, the way you can conduct a solid analysis, and how you can write answers that reflect the former two attributes.

WHAT TYPE OF LEARNER ARE YOU?

What is the best way for you to learn and study so that you retain the most information? Are you visual, kinaesthetic, or auditory? This theory of learning styles comes from the VAK model, a simple way to identify your best way of processing and understanding information. In order to retain and "get" new teachings some people need to hear information, some need to see, and some people need to actively tinker or touch things to learn best.

The easiest way to find out the answer is to search online for a free quiz. They usually range from 10-20 questions and can tell what your strongest suit is. Most of us are better at one and have a secondary learning trait. Mix the ideas from your top two styles together when developing your plan from the paragraphs below. The more tools that you have at your disposal the more likely it is that you will succeed. This information is the basis for your study plan and it will inform you on how to study for the test and how to prep for the rest of your future classes.

Once you figure out which style fits you then you can decide which tips and tricks are suited to your personal style. Don't waste a bunch of time making flowcharts if you are an auditory learner. Conversely, don't spend the majority of your time listening to lectures if your strongest asset is your ability to learn visually. Decide where to focus your energy to cut down on wasted study hours.

Study groups get into this rut all of the time because one member is a certain type of learner and inadvertently foists their style on others who may not benefit as much from a particular method. Make sure that if you work with a study group that everyone knows each others learning methods. Vary the learning tactics so that everyone gets a chance to work with the material and hear or see it presented their best way.

The following paragraphs give ideas for each type of learning style. Work with the ideas and tailor them to suit your needs.

VISUAL

Visual learners are generally able to learn tasks by taking in the information as a whole, this is manifested by a preference for charts and diagrams.

Lecture is less important to visual learners because it takes more effort and energy to understand what the professor is presenting. Writing notes and shorthand diagrams while the professor is talking helps. Sitting at the front of the class will keep your focus on the speaker and not wandering around the room. If you wish to listen to lecture during your study periods then it's advisable to watch video lectures so that you have someone to look at and get visual cues from.

A visual aesthetic is one that flows without interruption or pause. Its fluidity allows it to pass over drawn material and understand it but its water like qualities makes it skip over pertinent information like river rocks if it isn't presented correctly.

It's easy for a visual learner to "zone out" if you are just listening to lecture. Read the information that your professor is going to present before the class so that you go in with a good idea of what is happening before you even step in the door. It will keep you engaged in the material because it you will hear familiar concepts during the lecture and retain the ideas presented better. You spend hours everyday in class and this tactic will help you with recalling information better than just heading into a lecture cold.

When you study with a group make use of a chalkboard or whiteboard to present ideas. Flash cards can also be useful tools for visual learners. When you first crack open your dense casebooks and horn books you may have a moment where you feel overwhelmed because you are used to seeing information as a whole and legal books are too dense to give you that. A good practice for overcoming those dense blocks of texts is using pens and highlighters to separate the important information. Think about some more things that have helped you in the past and write them down.

AUDITORY

Auditory learners remember spoken directions best. Asking questions is a great tool for auditory learners to fully understand whats going on. So if you have a chatterbox in study group don't shut them out, it's their best method for learning. If you need to talk to understand then get with a like minded classmate and ask and answer each others questions. Verbally working through each issue will cement the points that you are learning.

Mnemonics are an auditory learner's best friend. You will have the capability to associate concepts to words and that is an invaluable thing to have during tests. Talk to yourself! In the shower, on walks, wherever you aren't disturbing other people who are studying you should verbalize the information that you are working on. If you cannot talk to yourself because you happen to be in a quiet space then move your lips while you think. Even the act of moving your lips will let you "hear" what you need to know.

You are a communicator tape your professor's lectures and listen to them later. Think about some more things that have helped you in the past and write them down. Talk to yourself, thinking aloud helps you work through a problem better than silently reading the same paragraph or page over and over again. Say out loud what you don't "get".

KINAESTHETIC LEARNING

The hands on approach suits you best. To begin developing your study plan you have to figure out how to allocate your hours because a stuffy library might not always be the best place for you to learn. You aren't a dreamer or a follower, you are a doer.

One of the best ways for you to practice is to develop a lesson plan for a subject and "teach" it to other people. You are an asset to your study group. Spend time preparing materials and really get into the idea of presenting, it will feel a lot less like studying and a lot more like you are actually getting things done.

Buy a whiteboard from an office supply store and write. Stand up, use your hands to write on the board, gesture and generally involve your whole body in the process. You will find that your type can learn a lot more by participating in the learning experience rather than passively listening to lecture or reading.

Move around when you study and take frequent, short breaks where you stand up and stretch. When you are done studying you might want to make a little time to exercise and go through what you just learned in your head. Get your blood pumping so your body and mind stay engaged.

Make diagrams with colors. Create your own charts. Flashcards are great because you have to create them, manipulate them, and shuffle them around. Think about some more things that have helped you in the past and write them down.

PUTTING THE PIECES TOGETHER

Once you figure out what works for you study wise then it's time to put the pieces together. You can't cram for your law exams or the FYLSX. The entire foundation of a solid legal education is built deliberately without haste. Your first goal after learning how you learn best is to develop a set plan that fits in all of your study hours, class hours, homework hours, and life in general hours.

Some people don't study effectively and figure that they will just take some professional prep courses at the end of the year. These professional courses cost hundreds and sometimes thousands of dollars but they aren't a panacea for lack of study and taking them certainly won't ensure that you pass. No one else can take this test with you, it's all about what you can fit into your head and carry into the test room.

HOW DO I STUDY?

Well first of all.....Don't consider what you are doing as just study. It's much more than that, it's also PRACTICE! When you are a lawyer you won't be studying cases, you are going to practice law. Approach your study hours as time to refine your knowledge and gain new insights so you will be a successful lawyer. School isn't about rote memorization and passive hours spent poring over books, it's about practicing the logical application of information. You have to spend a great deal of time developing these skills.

You have to develop a daily routine that takes all of your obligations into account. You may have to divide your time between work, family, leisure, and school. That's a lot of slices of pie to divide. Begin plotting your study program by grabbing planner or creating a document on the computer to block out some dedicated time.

Your academic career takes precedence over everything else at this point. Squeeze in at least a couple of hours a day for class and school. Getting enough information and skill to pass is going to take careful planning along with consistency.

What time do you learn best? Are you an early bird or a night owl? Do you get a second wind in the afternoon? You should be alert and available when it's time to get your work done. This may mean that you have to go to sleep an hour later or wake up an hour earlier but if you are dedicating yourself to law school then that's going to be your life for the next few years.

You might benefit from "second sleep" tactic because it's a way to steal back some time from a busy schedule. Understand that you will be running on a really tight schedule for the next few years. Your academic career is a major sacrifice, especially during the first year when there's so much pressure and the FYLSX to take into account. No matter how brilliant you are it's still a whole new language that takes time to master.

There's a theory on "second sleep" that has advantages when learning complex subjects. Second sleep or bimodal sleep is when you go to sleep for 3-4 hours then awaken after that period to study, read, or write. After an hour or two you put everything away and go back to sleep for several more hours and then go about your day normally upon awakening the second time.

There's an added benefit because the dead of the night is usually quiet and free from noise and intrusions. You don't turn on bright lights or hop out of bed and roam around. Open up your laptop or pull out a book and read with lights bright enough to see but dim enough so your brain doesn't think "wake up" for the day. The idea is to slip back into sleep naturally after the study period is over.

I study right before going to bed and the information uploads during the first half of my sleep process then upon awakening the material has had time to crystallize. This makes the middle of the night study period particularly effective because I'm not going in cold. Using this technique I've dreamed full papers, woken up, and written them without a pause and then gone back to sleep. You won't just eat and breathe law... you're going to dream it too!

In the beginning the time that you block out must be as free from the distractions of home and work life as possible. You need to have the quiet and space to find a rhythm and make school a habit. You can head to the library, coffee shop, school, or an empty park to find alone time. The first few months of study have to be quiet and focused. Adding in distraction later is a tool so that you can be ready for anything but the first few months are especially stressful and require some expert juggling skills to get a routine going.

You need the quiet right now because you are sitting down to learn how to read. Yes, you are going to learn how to read. The initial hours you spend with your casebooks and horn books are going to be incomprehensible because they are written in a manner unlike most other disciplines. They are dense and chock full of legalese not typically used in layman's books. You can dramatically cut down on the hours spent passively reading if you speed read the cases before you write selected briefs.

There are two things to remember about reading these big old books. First don't be intimidated by them. You will get the hang of reading these opinions, cases, and questions soon enough. And second, don't take the easy way and rely on the commercial outlines that break down the tough analysis. You have to learn how to crack open these books and synthesize this information without relying on others interpretation.

It's OK. to start off slowly, organizing your study plan and doing your assigned readings and definitions for the first weeks. In college the rule of thumb is three hours of study per one unit of credit starting from day one but in legal education that number has much more fluidity.

Your study hours will naturally ramp up as you become more familiar with the concepts, when more thinking and less memorization is required. The last month you will block out 9 hours for full practice tests at least once a week.

If you are not working full time then treat school as if it is your job and if you are working then make it your number one priority. You have to put in adequate out of class hours in order to do your very best.

There are a lot of negative attitudes about FYLSX success rates and Bar passage rates of non-ABA law students. All it takes is a quick Internet search to see a lot of cringe worthy comments. It's really not about capability; it's that it takes a lot of effort to get through law school and pass the exams required. If you are returning to school or working then that adds another level of difficulty.

Add in that non ABA students have to take the FYLSX and it becomes a real challenge. Too many students give up because they don't know how to approach the study of law in a productive manner or they don't put in the time to be successful. You don't have to pretend to study for ten hours a day like so many law students in top tier schools. Be pragmatic and study intelligently so that you can cut those hours down to just a few per day.

Law school is really nothing like undergrad and there are far less tools for us to access in a non-traditional setting. ABA students sign a contract where they promise not to work during their first year of school so they can devote enough time to study. The schools also tend to have additional support available because they are better funded (they charge students an arm and leg so they should be!) You have to live with the reality that things are not going to be easier for you, in fact, they will be harder. You might end up living off of caffeine and motivation. But if being a lawyer is for you then it's worth every bit of effort.

STUDENTS WHO ARE EMPLOYED FULL TIME

Those students who work full time need to be dedicated and commit to the upcoming rigors before going any further. You don't have any extra space to skip a week of studying and hit the books harder the next week. You are the tortoise in this race. Slow and steady is your course. Your path through this year is going to be different from the student who has plenty of free time.

You know yourself better than anyone else so keep in mind that these are just guidelines. You have to decide what a good balance is for you. There are people who have to work a little slower and need more time. There are others who can pack in an incredible amount of work in fewer hours. Block out between two to three hours per day to study on full time work days. On your days off or weekends bump it up to four to six hours depending on your class assignments.

Don't bother briefing cases besides the ones required by your professors. Your main focus is learning the concepts and definitions, not busy work. Later you will have to dedicate nine hour days near the finish line to take practice exams.

Use your spare time to keep abreast of the cases going on in the media and read the newspaper or reliable media sites. Read about lawyers that inspire you and the laws that are being enacted and argued about today. Inspire yourself.

If you are working in a position that accrues vacation time you should try to take some time off later in your studies to gear up for the test. Take some time off the before your test date and get a lot of quality work done. You will have learned a great deal by this point ion the year so study will be more about fine tuning the work that you already have learned. Too early and you risk not knowing enough law to effectively study, too late and you risk the temptation to cram right up to the test date.

FULL TIME STUDENTS

If you can dedicate your free time to academic pursuits then don't waste the advantage. Study four hours a day and an extra hour or so for reading outside sources that pertain to current events or law. This study is independent of your class assignments. Weekends are really going to be a blast from now on (just kidding), you will need to dedicate five to six hours of focused study in order to stay competitive. Don't feel overwhelmed by these numbers, it's not as bad as it sounds. If you are indeed a future lawyer these numbers are downright leisurely.

Keep abreast of the cases going on in the media and read the newspaper or reliable media sites. Read about lawyers and law. Supreme Court cases can make fascinating reading.

Discover who inspires you and read up on them via their books, cases, or articles. You can get one day off to recharge when you need it. I generally don't take too many of those though, being the best is more important than having rest. The lucky thing about being a full time student is that you do have extra hours to pursue hobbies or volunteer at a law firm or government agency. Get some hands on experience while you have the time.

GETTING DOWN TO BUSINESS: MONTHS 1&2

The first few weeks of class are about settling in and deciding what your academic calendar is going to look like for the semester. The first month of law school you have to get into the groove by listening intently during class, getting familiar with your syllabi, taking good notes, re-writing those notes during study, doing assignments, and familiarizing yourself with legal language by learning the definitions and immersing yourself in the legalese. Whew, that's already a lot of work. Work on your calendar and set up your schedule.

After the first month you should wade into the essays on your own if your professors haven't assigned any. Choose two or three from the Cal Bar website. Read them well and write a thorough analysis. Keep an eye on the time but don't pressure yourself. These essays won't be great but looking at them later in the year will show you just how far you have come. Do your best on these essays and toss them in a folder for review later.

During the first month there are a few more things that you can do to improve your academic success. Honestly assess your typing skills. If you hunt and peck at the keyboard to keep up with your thoughts then you will benefit from working with a typing program. There are many free online resources that can help, you don't have to learn to touch type but increasing your speed hasn't hurt anyone yet.

You have to write between 4,000 and 6,000 words in four hours to pass the FYLSX. Getting to that word count is essential and it requires that you write and edit simultaneously. You have to get your words out as fast as possible during the FYLSX and poking around for letters wastes time that you don't have. If you practice typing skills now then you won't have to worry later in the year. Your goal is to produce a fully fleshed out essay in the 1K to 1500 word range in an hour.

Take an unbiased look at your reading skills.

Are you a slow reader?

Did you struggle if you took the LSAT?

How is your reading comprehension?

Do you have to reread passages in order to understand what is being communicated?

Correct any issues ASAP. Law requires a great deal of reading dense packets of information. Processing information so you can remember and recognize similarities is what you need to learn.

Learning speed reading techniques is time well spent. There are inexpensive books that will give you a good start and, as always, Internet articles are a great resource to pick up ideas. Fact patterns can a turn a case with one word. Your Perry Mason moment may very well be when you catch an opaque exception in a fact pattern. When you read a pattern quickly with good comprehension it will help you catch those moments and keep you from making mistakes in your analysis .

You are going to hear a lot more about the **IRAC** method of writing in the coming months. Forget everything you've learned before, this is a whole new system and you will learn the ins and outs of it. Practice IRAC as soon as you begin writing essays, it's easier to create good habits from the start than to break bad ones later. People who are mathematics majors will revel in its formulaic simpleness, English majors may well just sit in a corner and wonder about their life choices. Its extremely formulaic but there is a method to the madness. At some point writing this way will be second nature to you but it's pretty alien at first.

Typically your professor will have given you a syllabus that tells you which pages in your casebook or horn book to read with each class lecture topic. Read and take notes based on the text before attending class. It doesn't matter what type of learner you are, you still have to do the pre-class reading and go fully prepared.

Before each class spend time thinking about the topics being presented. We all have some downtime during the day when we can think about the next class. Downtime in this context consists of activities where your mind can be active while performing mundane tasks. Showering, driving, washing dishes, the moments before falling asleep are all good times to really think. Do this for your upcoming lectures. You will get a lot more out of class if you are already acquainted with the material and actively considering any questions that you may have or that your Professor might ask. This is something that you will do for each class for the rest of your legal education and you will be a better student for it.

WHEN YOU STUDY MONTHS 1&2

- Have a commercial outline when you study. Buy Torts, Criminal, and Contract outlines and get familiar with them.

- Take along your notes from previous classes and reread them. Rewrite the parts that aren't clear or fresh.

- Write out your definitions. Eventually you will have a stack of notebooks that look like they were written by a mad person because you will have pages of the same definitions written over and over again. Don't worry about being neat; this is an exercise in muscle memory. The words will eventually come from your hands without pause. This takes lots of repetitive writing. There are hundreds of definitions to learn. Start this task early.

- Learn **IRAC** (Issue, Rule, Analysis, Conclusion)and practice writing your definitions as issues and rules so that you get the first two points of the format down. IRAC is your backbone for the essays.

- The quality of your study is more important than the amount of study. Sitting with a book propped on your lap while you play candy crush for four out of eight hours doesn't count as eight hours of study. Put the electronic devices down and focus.

- Take frequent (every hour or so), short breaks and pay close attention while you study.

- Read this book while you still have time for extra reading so that you get a full feel of what you need to do to prepare for the test.

MIDDLE MONTHS 3-6

You should be feeling less intimidated by your work load. You've hit a groove, but don't get too comfortable. When you're in class pay close attention. It's easy to feel less pressure at this point and slack off. You won't get this time back. Sometimes people realize that they haven't studied enough when it's too late, so keep plowing ahead.

Incorporate new techniques into your study routine to keep it fresh. Don't discontinue your other practices but limit the amount of outside reading that you do so you can work on some newer concepts. Acclimate yourself to harsher conditions and create mentally challenging opportunities.

WHEN YOU STUDY MONTHS 3-6

- The peace and quiet that you've gotten used to is just not the reality of test day. Now it's time to study at Starbucks, with the TV on, and on the subway. Vary the distraction level so you can study in any type of environment. When you sit for the real test people will cough, move chairs, get up, laptop keys are clacking, time is called by the proctors. Prepare so you won't be intimidated by the natural buzz that accompanies 700 stressed out people sitting in one big room.

- This does not mean that you should answer your phone, check e-mail, or Facebook during these study sessions.

- Create experiences that will teach you rapid decision making. There is no time to ruminate on theory and ponder legal issues during the FYLSX. The experience of taking timed essays allows you make mistakes before the FYLSX where one poor essay and a few mediocre ones can send you to the bottom of the pile. Practice by taking the full eight hour test experience with a one hour break once to see how it feels.

- Trade your timed essays with other students and grade each others work. Look at issue spotting, IRAC format, syntax, and analysis. Take the criticism and use it to advance your work. Don't be defensive or emotional about this. The essays that you send out and the essays you grade will likely be poor in the beginning. Don't feel shame or anger, instead feel proud that you have made it this far.

- Practice MBE's and get into writing essays in earnest. Multi-choice questions will join your commercial outlines as your best friends. Don't sit down and do a bunch of them at once though. Start with doing sets of ten questions and really deconstruct the fact patterns in them.

- Ditch the laptop on some days and do old school studying. Low key study habits give you a boost because it forces your hands to become more active and slows the writing process down. You hands write slower than you think. This isn't ideal for the test but it's great for study conditions where retention rules over speed. Make a bag with pens, highlighters, notepads, and hit the good old fashioned books.

- Print out essays and model answers from the Cal Bar and carry them with you in a folder. Write your own essay answers and then check your work against the model essays. Did you spot all of the issues? If you didn't then what clues in the pattern did you miss? This is a quick activity that you can do on a lunch break.

- Learn how to format the essays so that they are what the Bar is looking for visually. This means an IRAC format with bolding and underlining at appropriate places. Develop good habits now so that they stick with you. The Bar is looking for a specific structure, they are not interested in originality. Go with the proven formula. IRAC works. It's proven by how many model answers follow it.

THE FINAL STRETCH

You've hit your stride. If you haven't been making huge gains then now its time chart your progress. Take some time to suss out any problem areas if you find yourself struggling. Learning is a process and you always have to reassess and see what is and what isn't working for you. Are your study times still working for you? Is it time to readjust your learning techniques?

Before you do though, look back over your essays and MBE's that you tucked away a few months ago. Bask in your success for a minute. You have essays that show marked progress and you should be a veteran of the great MBE wars in months three through six.

You should have notebooks filled to the brim with your garbled handwriting and a raging caffeine addiction to rival Voltaire's. Balzac himself was a great connoisseur of the stuff saying "Coffee glides into one's stomach and sets all of one's mental processes in motion. One's ideas advance in column of route like battalions of the Grande Armée......The artillery of logic thunders along........... The characters don their costumes, the paper is covered with ink, the battle has started, and ends with an outpouring of black fluid like a real battlefield enveloped in swaths of black smoke from the expended gunpowder. Were it not for coffee one could not write, which is to say one could not live."

Between staying alert, active, and focused you should be doing well. If not then reassess. Start at the beginning and discover what you need. If you ask your professors they will likely take a short meeting with you to discuss your deficits in their class.

The home stretch is about refining your study regimen. Become an expert in the subjects that you know and become competent in the areas that you find most difficult.

WHEN YOU STUDY: THE FINAL STRETCH

- Go over every published FYLSX essay so that you know the types of questions that they typically ask. Write as much as you actually need to, if you are a strong writer then use your writing time elsewhere. You must read them all though, along with the model answers. Make sure that your IRAC formatting is on point.

- Time to memorize case names for each area so that you can buttress your arguments with cases during the essay portion. The Hand formula (calculus of negligence), *Palsgraf v LIRR*, etc. You are going to have a lot more opportunities to memorize specific cases in contract and tort law than in criminal. Criminal requires knowledge of common law v modern law, the various insanity tests, etc. Make some flashcards with the case names on one side and the type of law and a few particulars regrading the case on the reverse.

- Trade essays with classmates or those in your study group and grade each other ruthlessly. There is no room for hurt feelings in this exercise. If done correctly it will allow you to see new areas in which to improve your technique. Spotting other peoples mistakes and seeing their talents will also let you see where your own strengths and weaknesses lay.

- Don't stop with the MBE's. You will carefully dissect these up until the days before the test. Do several full 100 mock MBE exams to make sure that your timing is good. Two days before the exam drop everything and relax.

- Don't forget everything that you have been doing for the months prior. The above list simply states things that you should add to your routine. This is what I mean about ramping up the studying.

HELP! I HAVE NO TIME TO STUDY

Many students in non ABA schools choose this educational model option because of time constraints. Families, jobs, relationships, and other obligations are typical of many students who choose this road less traveled. This is no reason or excuse to expect that this is a less mentally rigorous route. In fact, you are a credit to the non ABA model if you complete Law school, pass the Bar and practice quality law. We all take the same Bar and practice in the same courts. Your Professors may understand your obligations but the Bar doesn't care so you had better be prepared. Here are a few tips to help you get out of the "no time" rut:

- Work around your work. Instead of lunch breaks use them as study breaks. Take your books with you and get in 30 minutes. Pack a quick lunch for your break and find a quiet spot to read or work essays.

- Print out a few essays at a time from the Cal Bar past essay page and take them everywhere with you. You can't make time but you can steal time back from the little things that waste your precious minutes. If they are close at hand you can pull them out and give them a quick review anytime you are waiting around somewhere.

- Remember that on certain days you may not have a couple of hours to study. This doesn't mean that your minutes aren't just as valuable. It also doesn't mean that you study double the next day, which can lead to burnout. Use whatever time that you have and don't stray from your routine the next day.

- Streamline your wasted minutes: delete the extraneous apps on your phone and go dormant on social media. These little distractions can take up a lots of time in little increments. TV is also verboten, if you can't find the time to study then forget about your favorite show. Your friends, games, and TV shows will still be there after you take the FYLSX.

- Download all the free and low cost legal apps that you can. Use these apps on your phone or tablet instead of playing games or texting. Instead of scrolling through social media while in line at the grocery store or at the DMV pull out your phone and review questions, listen to lectures, or look at outlines on your new legal apps.

- Take the subway or bus to and from work or school. The time that you can steal from driving and pour into reading, outlining, or reviewing is invaluable. If public transport is not possible then pop a CD in your car or have lectures downloaded onto your device and listen to lecture while you drive. Even if you aren't primarily an auditory learner it's still better than not utilizing this time.

- In the shower recite the definitions, you may find it more difficult than writing them. Press yourself to the max. Having to recall and verbalize the information is harder than it seems.

STUDY GROUPS

There are positives and negatives with study groups. Sometimes students "save up" their studying until they meet with the group. There's also a lot of coordination involved for scheduling meeting times/places. Groups that aren't well run have a tendency to reinforce bad information and bad habits via hive mind. However, they also reinforce a good group dynamic. It's nice to work with others. Sometimes we get into study "blind spots" miss a particular weakness. A good group with members who offer constructive criticism is an asset. Stay cognizant of the potential pitfalls and a study group may be a good tool in your arsenal.

If you do enter into a study group arrangement then make sure that it aligns with your particular needs and that everyone's educational goals are being met. It's not meant to be an arrangement of friends who get together to gossip and chit chat with a little bit of law talk included. Make a firm schedule and limit study group hours to no more than 20% of your total study hours.

There are a few different ways to allocate study group hours. You can use the time as a teaching forum where everyone prepares a presentation and delivers a short 10-15 minute lecture teaching the group the subject. The "teacher" then has to answer questions. Everyone goes around and teaches their subject one at a time. It's a method that will introduce subjects to the group and the "teacher" learns the subject thoroughly because they have to be prepared to field any question or scenario.

Another method is more of a quiet study method; sometimes it's just nice to be in a room with everyone sharing the same struggle. You all sit down and independently study but there is a group goal. Say "assignments and delegations" and after an hour or two of study everyone comes together to discuss the subject. Doing the "five/ten questions" MBE exercise discussed later is also beneficial when amplified in a group. You get a lot more questions done. Have each person do five MBE questions and then discuss them all as a group.

If your study group is composed of different types of learners each type should present to the group via their specialty. Two auditory learners could present to the group with a Q& A session. Visuals could create a PowerPoint presentation. Kinetics can show off some poster board diagrams, mnemonics, or charts that they designed. It's a great way to mix up the monotony of study and introduce different tactics to each other.

Talk to a few classmates or study group partners and set up an essay trade. Pick a couple of essays from the past exam page of the California Bar website. Write in timed conditions an essay and trade essays for grading either in person or email. Then make an agreement that feelings are not involved in this process and invite constructive criticism. It's a lot better to hear some helpful critique than it is to get a notice that you failed the test.

Really listen to the criticism and offer helpful hints to them as well. Was it easy to read? Was the law correct? Were all the issues spotted? Is it formatted properly, written in complete sentences, and spell checked? Was the word count at an appropriate level? Was the analysis thorough? A peer evaluation isn't perfect but having fresh eyes look at your work is always a great idea.

FINAL THOUGHTS ON STUDYING

When you are not doing the basics or if you get burned out pick up a couple of books on legal theory. Buy at least one in each subject so that you can see the ideas and concepts that run underneath the law. Ask why things are the way they are. When you study cases look at both sides of the question. You should be able to take any case and argue either side using good law.

If there's one mantra that has served me well it's this: No days off and no excuses. Once I took that advice to heart everything became much clearer and focused. That doesn't mean that you won't get tired or bored, trust me, you will. It just means that you have to keep going despite boredom and exhaustion.

If you pick up your book and realize that you simply cannot go over another negligence outline or the thought of spending even one minute on products liability is enough to cause hives don't slam the book shut and take the day off. Do something else, the schedule that you create is a guideline and human beings are flexible and fluid. Work on contracts or criminal or if all of it is giving you the shivers pick up a theory book or just kick back, close your eyes and listen to a few lectures. Maybe you need to take an hour to organize your study material for the next session. This is to make sure that you that there are no excuses and no outs to keep you from doing the work that you have committed yourself to. Would you want a surgeon who coasted through school or a lawyer without passion? I wouldn't.

That being said, we all have busy lives and have to keep this work at the forefront. It's very rare to meet someone who is able to take months off and sequester themselves in order to study for the FYLSX. That's why it is imperative that you find times to study where you can maximize your benefit in the shortest amount of time possible. It's your personal drive that will keep you going during the hard times. Those hard times are the when you are sleepy, or want to relax, or swamped at work. Personal crises are always a part of life. Write out your five year goals and whenever you are feeling low or unmotivated reread them. Things like that are gas for your journey.

After you have taken the test take a couple of days off... Hug your friends and family and thank them for being supportive. Go out a few times and enjoy life and then....... hit the books again. Pass or fail you are still going to need all this info for the Bar so it certainly doesn't hurt to keep your head immersed in the law. The subjects that you are learning now are the foundation for most of your future classes. But you can definitely ease up and cut your studying down dramatically based on how well you think you did.

As you can see, none of the things that make good student habits are superhuman qualities and anyone who has the ability to participate in a JD. program can learn these skills, and become a good lawyer. But it does take practice, discipline, and focus. The test is just a hurdle that you have to leap before moving on to the next part of the law school race. Now it's time to take a look at each part of what will make you a top performer.

CHAPTER 3: THE FOUNDATION: LEARNING THE DEFINITIONS

So what are legal definitions and why are they important? Simply put, the definitions are single sentence descriptions of each term. Battery, assault, intent, causation, negligence, assignment, consideration, and hundreds other common words have a precise legal meaning that includes all of the elements of the law pertaining to it. The words that you see above are common in the English language but mean something completely different when used in the law. Each one has a specific legal definition that bears little resemblance to their Webster's dictionary counterpart.

Have a handle on proper language, legal and otherwise. Learning legal vocabulary is a cornerstone and having your definitions memorized perfectly is important because if you miss an element in a definition it can change the whole issue that you are working on. If someone is claiming common law burglary (The trespassory breaking and entering into the dwelling place of another, at night, with the intent to commit a felony therein) and the fact pattern shows that the crime was committed during the day then common law burglary must be raised in the essay and rejected using clear analysis because of the missing element. If you have forgotten that "nighttime" element then you will erroneously apply common law burglary as a chargeable offense and have an incorrect analysis and conclusion.

You have to get to the point that you can type, write, or recite each element of a definition accurately and quickly. If someone walks up to you and says, "Hey, what's an offer?" You should be able to write down or recite "a manifestation of present contractual intent, communicated to the offeree, with definite and certain terms inviting acceptance" immediately, without pausing for a second. This goes for all of the new words that you will encounter throughout each subject.

You need to spend time getting to know these definitions perfectly. The mental dictionary that you create in your head is the basis for your legal reasoning and what you will use to analyze facts during the essays. There are hundreds of definitions to learn so get on this task as soon as you start school and keep it up until a few days before the test. There's no shortcuts on this part because you will also need to keep these definitions stored for the Bar.

Right now you may be wondering, "how do I memorize all of that information?" Well first, separate the broad categories, the lists, from the simple stand-alone definitions. The lists include the intentional torts, defenses to formation, defenses to murder, specific intent crimes, another for general intent crimes and several other categories that you will learn along the way. Take these lists and create mnemonics to help you remember. Your professors probably have good mnemonics. It's also pretty fun to make up your own. It will help your recall if they stand out for you. These are mental file folders to carry the definitions that fit into them.

For example intentional torts:

ABCFITT- assault, battery, conversion, false imprisonment, intentional infliction of emotional distress, trespass to chattel, and trespass to land.

Once you know *ABCFITT* you learn the definition for assault then battery and so forth until you have each one down. In the end you know that each one is in a folder called Intentional Torts-ABCFITT and you can pull up ech definition mentally as needed.

These broad categories keep everything in their place and assist you when it's time to begin your analysis. If all the defenses to intentional torts are in a single file in your brain then you won't fumble around when you write essays and potentially mix up an intentional tort defense with a negligence defense. Once you have the categories grouped then it's time to move further into the definitions.

My legal writing professor had us memorize ten to fifteen definitions per week and then take a quiz. That doesn't sound like much until you realize that some definitions can span a paragraph and the memorization is cumulative, even when you've memorized every single one that you need that week you will still have to be able to recall all of the others. This is an excellent approach to begin your study.

Take a commercial outline and write out the words that are in bold. Over time you will get to know the concepts behind the law and you can word your own definitions without using the rote memorization, but that takes time and during the test it's best to have your definitions memorized so you don't have to think about them.

CHAPTER 4: GETTING YOUR HANDS ON THE NECESSARY MATERIAL....... CHEAP!

You've got to become familiar with your school's library and the public law libraries located in most cities. Law librarians tend to be very accommodating and knowledgeable so it's great to go down there and learn the layout. But it's imperative to build your own personal library. It's not always feasible to visit the library and you can highlight and mark your personal books. Besides, you can't lay around in your pajamas at the library eating chips and reading. They don't like it much.

You shouldn't have just a book or two for each subject. Having an abundance of material in your personal legal library prevents that feeling of "book fatigue." That's the feeling that creeps up when you've been reading the same book for so long that you're thinking that the whole Fahrenheit 451 burning books concept wasn't such a bad idea. Additionally, when confusing material is presented in a variety of different ways and explained by different authors it tends to become clearer.

There were many times during my study when I sat on the floor and spread out four, five, or even nine books opened to the same concept just to read it multiple ways. It sounds cumbersome but it's actually a very efficient way to understand the material because of the different presentations.

You're going to need books. Lots and lots of books. Make space on your bookshelf and nightstand because the more resources that you have the more solid your understanding will be. Good books are the cornerstone of any good autodidacts library and law is the ultimate exercise in self disciplined study.

The problem with building an expansive legal library, besides shelf space, is money. It's nearly impossible to have a solid personal library full of 200 dollar books. That would cost thousands. I was on an extremely limited budget that precluded me from heading to the book store and picking up the full priced versions. In fact, I only paid full price for one legal book during 1L and it was an $11.99 paperback called "Plain English for Lawyers". You can get quality materials for a low price if you know where to look and invest time.

FINDING INEXPENSIVE MATERIALS

Your professors will put a book on the syllabus called "So and So's Contracts" 11th Edition." They often want you to buy the edition that they recommend because it jibes perfectly with their book. Ask your professor how far back you can go edition wise and still be on track, any missing cases can be photocopied or read at the main library.

Because bar issues don't change dramatically and because most of the information needed will still be in earlier editions it's a good idea to buy an older, cheaper book. The bulk of what you need will be in the less expensive editions; it just takes a few more minutes to make sure that you aren't missing a newer case that was added to the current one. Buying discounted books isn't difficult. Listed below are different ways to get a hold of low cost books and outlines.

However, you do have to get used to reading books that have been highlighted or otherwise lightly marked by others. But if they are otherwise undamaged you should try to get over it. Personally, I have learned how to live with a highlighted book. Buying them offers discounts of up to 99% (I've bought many one dollar case books from the thrift shop.) Also, buy what you can when you can. I've bought books a full year and a half before taking the class.

Amazon.com-

This is the Mecca of reasonably priced books. Amazon has great selection of used books sold by third party vendors as well as new books. It takes a little bit of digging and going for, say, a 5th or 6th edition versus a 7th edition. But since the law, for Bar purposes, doesn't change drastically they work just fine. Shipping on these third party books is generally 3.99 and you can come out with a ton of great books for under ten bucks each. Order early and expect to wait a week or two for each book. Look for cheap prep books, commercial outlines, casebooks, horn books, and even commercial flashcards here.

Thrift stores-

Thrift stores are a goldmine for used law books. They are usually priced at a couple of dollars each. Look for stores like Goodwill and Out of the Closet located in areas near big law schools. Make regular visits and ask the staff to let you know when a donation of law books arrives. They are generally flush with these books after the Bar results are released and at the end of the semester. Students need to make room for their incoming texts and J.D.s who have passed the Bar are usually happy to get those prep books out of their sight once and for all.

Network-

Talk to lawyers that you know and upperclassmen in your school. Many of them are willing to sell or give away books that they no longer have a use for.

Free Outlines-

There are plenty of people online who share their outlines although you have to be careful about any errors in them. Typically the more law student outlines say the same thing the more likely that it's good info. Student's put their outlines up all over the internet. It's an easy way to look at the information written differently. You will also be pleasantly surprised to see how uniform legal education is. A Stanford outline is the same as a People's College of Law outline in the same subject.

California Bar Website-

The Bar publishes the Essay questions from the FYLSX and the Bar in their "future lawyer" section. Print out these essays and work on them. Look at the model answers and compare your writing with what the Bar has selected. These essays are your guideposts to what the Bar expects from you and it's a free way to fill your folder with study material.

Other Books and Articles to Look For:

These are plenty of books that aren't required reading but are going to help you now and in the future. These particular types of books give you a range of tools to keep in your arsenal. If you don't run into any inexpensive books on these subjects then look to the Internet for good articles outlining the steps. Reading various memory, language, vocabulary, logic, and comprehension books in your downtime will streamline your thinking and make you a faster learner.

Memory books-

Mastering your memory requires that you learn how it works first and second how to use it to your best advantage. Some of the practices seem fairly cumbersome in the beginning but after a little practice it's amazing how much information you can cram into the space between your ears. Mnemonics, chunking, connecting information, and pegging are techniques that you can use regularly to improve retention.

Speed reading-

There are plenty of articles on the internet on this subject. You can also pick up books from thrift shops or Amazon. If reading quickly isn't one of your skills then it's going to be a definite deficit in your studies. You just want to make sure that you don't lose comprehension as your speed goes up. It shouldn't take too much time to read up on this subject so you can absorb the law and get through the reading quickly and efficiently.

Vocabulary Books-

You need to have a complete grasp of the English language and a major part of that is having an extensive vocabulary. Not everything you write requires you to use big words but you should know what they mean as many judges and lawyers enjoy sprinkling their writing with obscure terms. It also imbues your writing with a professional air when you can choose just the right word.

CHAPTER 5: STRATEGIES FOR THE MULTI CHOICE QUESTIONS

So now we are onto the MBE section of your study plan. Well, not quite. They aren't called MBE questions on the FYLSX. They are called MCQ's (Multi Choice Questions) and they are structured slightly different, but you will have work with standard Bar MBE's.

You are going to have to practice using MBE's because that's what is available. The Bar releases these questions fairly regularly so there are thousands of them to work with. Barbri and many other companies use these "released questions" in their materials, these are problems that were on actual Bar exams and have been retired. You will learn how the Bar examiners word the questions and you will run into most of the possible scenarios if you work with enough questions. When you train your brain to recognize the keywords and fact structures then you make it easier to apply the rules to any question with similar variables.

However, be prepared for the differences in the MCQ's. When you get to the FYLSX the booklet will tell you that there may be more than one correct answer for each question. This is tricky because you have to choose the best answer. It can be disconcerting to open the test booklet for the first time and see that. Just stay mentally prepared, read carefully and quickly, and tick off whatever elements are needed to answer the question. There is one set of official MCQ questions that was released by the FYLSX in 1980 and although there aren't many, only 100 questions, it's still useful to get a copy and go through them. They are available online so that you can have a general idea of how the questions are worded and what the best answers look like.

HOW TO STUDY THE MULTI CHOICE QUESTIONS

The worst thing to do when you begin practicing the MBE's is to sit down and push through fifty or a hundred questions. When you study don't zip right through the multiple choice questions just because the actual FYLSX is a timed test. Read slowly and analyze the questions word for word because that buildup will end up turning into rapid analysis later in the year. Don't wait until you know each and every rule and theory before practicing the MBE's.

Start with ten questions. Read each question and all of the answers then apply each answer to the question before eliminating what doesn't fit. Take your time, read slowly for comprehension, and practice picking out the buzzwords. Take a few minutes per question, well over the time the Bar allows. When you're done with the ten flip to the back of the book and see how you fared.

Keep your notebook handy after you grade because then begins the task of hand writing the correct answer and WHY it's the right answer. All of the MBE books give a brief analysis in the back. Reading this analysis allows you to see the process and understand how they arrived at the correct answer. Write out the answers multiple times for the questions that you got wrong or guessed at and just once for the ones that you got right. Ten questions done this way should take no less than an hour. If you are in line somewhere or have a few minutes to spare take that opportunity to do one or two questions.

This activity is going to help you with not just the MBE's but with the essays as well. You just don't want to skimp on understanding. What elements did you miss? Were there any red herrings? Writing out what you did right and what you did wrong will improve your analysis and knowledge of the elements. Rushing through and hitting time marks come later, after you have assimilated enough knowledge from this practice.

As we discussed above, the FYLSX has a different style of multiple choice question. They aren't like the regular MBE questions that you will study during this year but they aren't radically different either. The Bar has, to date, only released one series of their proprietary MCQ questions and they are from the 1980 test. Study the MBE's religiously, deconstruct them, think of them as mini fact patterns. Think like a lawyer. Why would you choose one answer over the other answer? What principles apply? Speed comes after skill, so first learn the different mechanisms that go into choosing a correct answer.

Once you've done several hundred MBE's in the above fashion you will start to feel ready for timed tests. The more questions that you do the better prepared you will be because you will have a trained mind and the ability to pick apart questions effectively. There is only a limited amount of ways that an issue can fit into a question. Specific actions, names, traits, and scenarios that compose the flesh of the questions will change but most key issues are presented similarly. What stays the same are the rules that are cloaked within these questions, if you can pick them out then you are on the right track. Even the smallest exception to the rules are obvious when you have prepared with enough questions.

DURING THE TEST

When the proctor gives you the go ahead to begin the FYLSX take a deep breath, start to work, and don't pause until you are finished. Read the call of the question (the last line with the question mark at the end) and then read all of the answers. After that read the fact pattern so that you have an idea of what you need to look for in the question. In fact, there were a few questions that were answerable just from reading the call and the A-D options.

If you are reading MCQ's for the first time then it will be stressful to see questions with multiple "correct" answers. They are not asking you to do anything but choose the BEST answer. Just like in life, there may be more than one correct answer in a scenario but only one is the best. You must base this on your own estimation of the pattern and the optimal solution to the presented problem.

This is where they test analysis. This idea of "best" differs wildly from the Barbri and other Bar methods where the process of elimination can get you far. This is where your definitions will sit beside you as faithful friends once again. Use your scratch paper or test booklet to run through the elements as needed. If one element is lacking then eliminate the possibility, do this without hesitation or equivocation, if it simply does not fit then there is no reason to spend another second entertaining the possibility.

When you run into the inevitable stumper question don't leave the answer box unfilled. Narrow it down, fill it, and then put a light mark next to it. If you have time after you are finished, return to it and see if you still feel like you made the best choice. Never walk away from an answer unfilled... even if it is a tentative decision it's still better than risking a royal screw-up because you skipped a beat. Don't get to the last question and realize that your answers are misaligned. Put a lightly (LIGHTLY) penciled star or dot next to it and return if time allows. Don't do this for as many as you like or feel uncertain of, only do this for the extreme circumstances. You shouldn't have more than three to five of these light marks by the end of the exam.

I think most people agree that your first instinct is usually the best instinct. Sometimes there is a visceral, unconscious reaction to something in the fact pattern that leads your hand to a certain bubble. Mark that bubble. This isn't about flipping coins or superstition but there is so much information presented to a 1L that it would be nearly impossible to track it all down via your conscious brain. You may have well had a reaction to something that you have learned before and stored in your busy brain. Mark it and consider yourself done with the question.

MCQ's can be tricky and sometimes things just seem like they are criminal or tortious when they are legally neither. It's a play on your emotions. One example is an omission where life is imperiled or lost but no true legal obligation exists as there was no duty due to lack of relationship, contract, act, etc. Those one's make you pause because certain things just feel morally wrong even if they are perfectly legal. Go by the letter of the law, not personal ethics.

Don't read so quickly that you gloss over facts and issues but certainly don't read slowly. You have a little over a minute and a half for each question so time is of the essence. If you have practiced speed reading and comprehension exercises then you should be fine.

Consume the call of the question and the answers before digesting the facts. Read the call of the question then the A. B.C. D. answers first so that when you read the actual fact pattern you are clicking the potential answers into place or discarding them. You will see exactly where the question is lacking in a certain element if you read the answers and calls first because you aren't glossing over any pertinent facts when you read the pattern; you have an idea of what you are looking for.

CHAPTER 6: HOW TO APPROACH THE ESSAYS

Timing and essay construction is where you should focus in the months leading up to the exam. Writing between 4,000-6,000 words in a four hour period takes some practice. Try different timing techniques to determine what produces consistent writing. Reread the Bar questions; the advantage of knowing what types of questions are asked and how long the test is means that you can drill until your timing is perfect.

There's really no excuse not to prepare adequately for the four hours of essays. They are, after all, a determining factor on whether or not you can continue in law school. I have a specific formula for tests and essay that works wonderfully for me. There are many other ways to work the essays as well and it's a matter of determining what suits you best. Most plans require some adjustments to fit individual tastes and abilities and it's prudent to begin those tweaks early on.

Essays are a difficult to gauge in terms of evaluating potential scores. There are certain rules and a good classmate or study group grader can tell you whether or not it is a "passing" essay or not but it really is pretty subjective. It's not like they can tell you with certainty whether a particular essay warrants a 70 vs. a 75. With MBE's at least you know for certain whether or not you are right when you practice.

This means that you have to hit every issue that you can in your hour. Analyze anything that seems relevant to the facts in the case and present it in a well formatted fashion. Every point counts. Issue spotting drills will teach you how to pull the relevant issues quickly. Speed and accuracy is your friend.

The problem that most students experience is learning and implementing the IRAC formula in every instance. It's a formula that is required to pass the Baby Bar, your finals, and the Bar exam in every state. It seems terribly redundant and most people feel a natural aversion to repeating words in a written form but that is what the test demands.

The whole idea is to assess your needs. If you are a slow writer or need to practice issue spotting and analysis you should spend time testing yourself using Bar essays at least three times a week after the first month of initial study. If you are a proficient writer you should do so once every two weeks or as needed. The extra time can be spent on advanced memorization, learning theory, and perfecting anything else that needs your attention.

Study the Model answers that the Bar releases after each exam. In the Past Exam section they give essays for the last 5 years along with two model answers per question. You can also look up plenty of past answers and questions that people have archived from many years past.

They aren't perfect because they are written by students, not professors or graders but they are representative of what the Bar is looking for. It will give you a good idea of what an answer is supposed to look like because one thing they all have in common is good formatting and the use of IRAC.

Formatting is one of the most important parts of your essay because if it looks professional the graders will likely look at it favorably. Dress your essay like it's going on a job interview. Crisp, formal, and well crafted. Make your essay pleasing to the eye and easy for the readers to skim because they aren't going to spend much time reading it and they certainly won't go hunting for your salient points.

Graders typically spend just a couple of minutes reading the essay that you painstakingly crafted and your four essays don't all go to the same grader. They are distributed to multiple graders so make sure that you format each one so that they are easy to read. The issues need to **be BOLD and <u>UNDERLINED</u>**. If your essay looks good then you have already won a part of the essay battle. Put your cases in ***bold italics (Sullivan v NY Times)*** so that they stand out. Keep lots of "white space" in your answers to break up the text blocks into digestible portions.

Keep your paragraphs short. Three to five sentences is standard. Reading a ton of essays on the same subject is exhausting so if your issues **POP** the grader won't skip over it and possibly miss your issue and analysis.

Use your new legal language correctly but don't veer into using overly complex legalese just because you want to show your big vocabulary. Buzz words are going to carry your analysis along, not long 50 cent words that you pick up in life. Avoid turgid sentences that hide your point in a muddle of useless words. The graders are skimming the essays for content and bloated sentences hide valid analysis.

Reasonable, foreseeable, mens rea, actus reus, intent, malice….. All of these words have special legal meaning and those are the words that you should use liberally in your work. Even if it feels redundant it lets the grader know that you understand the concepts that they expect you to know.

In order to craft a well-built essay you have to:

1.read the fact pattern and find what issues are relevant.

2. Analyze the issues use the facts to buttress your argument using logic and direct quotes from the pattern.

3. Let your entire analysis procedure play out on the page. Why did you come to the conclusion that you did? Use simple language but be thorough. You came to the conclusion z because of y reason because of a, b,c facts. Type all of that out so the graders can see your process. In math it's called "showing your work."

TIMING YOUR ESSAYS FOR THE EXAM

It is the trade of lawyers to question everything, yield nothing, and talk by the hour. -Thomas Jefferson

The quote above succinctly states what the essays are all about. You need to question everything in the fact pattern and analyze it thoroughly. Why are certain sentences there? Everything in the fact pattern is put there for a purpose. Once you find the threads in the fact pattern that point to your conclusion you follow them while discussing and possibly dismissing the other available conclusions.

Once again, you only have an hour per essay. Way back when everyone was hand writing for the Bar and the FYLSX the standard was to read the question once, read it again while underlining, spend 15 minutes writing an outline, and only then did one begin to write. Since most test takers are using laptops now it seems redundant to do so. Writing the issues directly into the Bar program saves a great deal of time. I list all of the issues first and then dive directly into writing within the first five minutes.

I adhere to a firm 45 minute essay time line. Resist the urge to flip open the exam booklet and read all of the questions before settling on the one that you like. There is nothing to be gained from cherry picking the essays and there is a lot to lose. Namely your two greatest commodities: confidence and time.

Begin at number one, spend 45 minutes writing and then turn the page, You're going to have to complete them all of the essays so don't bother trying to get an "easy" one out of the way first, that's what the extra hour at the end is for. So you can go back, polish and refine. I spent only about five more minutes on what I thought was my worst essay (scored at 70) and twenty more minutes on my best (scored at 80). I divvied up the rest here and there. The big advantage to this system is that when you skim back over the fact pattern a few more issues that you missed the first go round should jump out. You have given yourself breathing room and the topic has crystallized in your head while you were working on the other essays.

Read the question once using pencil to underline any buzz words or issues. Then write the relevant issues directly into the Exam Pro software in order of what they are. Then begin writing. When I took the test I was shocked at how many people were sitting there scribbling on scratch paper for 10-15 minutes before even touching their computer. Then they had to transcribe that outline into the computer. What a waste of time! Use the scratch paper sparingly.

Start writing within three minutes of opening the test booklet so that you can get those bold issues down. Read the question with your pencil in hand and mark or underline any buzzwords or issues. List all the issues that you have spotted directly into the Exam Pro software. **Bold and underline** the issues so they don't get lost and so they are already formatted.

Then reread the question to scoop up whatever you missed on the first issue grab. If you see "products liability" then type that and each other subsequent issue that you spot. Buzzwords are clues, they indicate that an issue is likely to exist. They include action words or dates that could raise potential issues.

After the second read through you should have a list of bold, underlined issues. Go to the first issue and write your definition, write it quickly and don't miss any elements. This is why it is imperative that you develop that muscle memory and have each definition mentally accessible. There really isn't time to pause and ponder during this step.

Keep an eye on the time and begin writing your analysis. Look back at your copy of the question and use quotes and words from the pattern to buttress your arguments. This is the most important part of the essay so make it coherent and logical. Use short sentences with basic structure so that your argument is easy to follow. Remember, you are doing all of this in the short span of 45 minutes from beginning to end. Hit all the issues that you listed. Stop writing as soon as the 45 minutes is up. Don't continue a moment longer.

Now turn the page and do this for the next question. At the end of the four sets of 45 minutes you will have an entire hour to spare. Turn back to the first essay and reread the question. If you divide the time equally you have 15 minutes per essay to add analysis and refine your work. There are many benefits to this extra period. Leaving the question to ruminate in your head for that time will allow you to improve the analysis and you will likely pull out some extra issues and that can be added. Your argument will be more developed and nuanced when you go back over it. You now also know what your best essay is and what your worst essay likely is.

There are four essays and not each one will be equally strong for you. Spend some more time on your best essay and make it shine. The fact pattern is better fixed in your mind and it's also easier to write when the sword named "finish me" is no longer dangling over your head. You now have four complete essays. OK, they aren't one hundred percent complete, but they are good enough to give you some space and let you breathe while tightening up your remaining work. I really believe that this method is what got me a published answer. Going back to an answer that is already "done" takes a great deal of pressure off and I was able to polish it and add some good stuff.

Hit spell check. This is pretty self-explanatory but, for some reason, a lot of people neglect to spend the extra minute per essay to tighten up their work. Points are not supposed to be deducted for misspelled words but in the real world we know that presentation matters. In an hour you wont be sending in your best possible essay but at least it won't be sloppy work.

WORD COUNT FOR THE ESSAYS

Time is not all that counts when crafting essays. The length and word count are also indicators of whether or not an essay is passing. If you write too little then you are missing issues or lacking in analysis, both are fatal flaws. Conversely, if you are writing very long essays then you are using too much filler or skimping on the other three essays to overwrite one. Considering that there are only four hours to complete the essays it's important to manage your word counts during essay writing practice so that it isn't difficult to fall in the perfect range during test day.

A good essay touches all the points in 1000-1500 words. Shoot for those counts. Below are the model essay word counts for the last two June baby bar administrations. As you can see they all fall into the range with just a couple of exceptions.

June 2014

- A 1,057, B 968

- A 1,620, B 1,492

- A 1537, B 2960

- A 1856, B 1055

June 2013

- A 1334, B 1030

- A 1124, B 1379

- A 895, B 1268

- A 1467, B 1410

HOW TO WRITE FOR THE EXAM

The minute you read something that you can't understand, you can almost be sure that it was drawn up by a lawyer. -Will Rogers

That adage certainly used to be true years ago but modern lawyers are trending towards creating engaging, readable documents and reviews. Essay writing should be interesting and coherent as well.

Legal writing is, in essence, basic long-form syllogistic writing and it takes a bit of getting used to. The IRAC format that is the basis of your legal essays requires practice. Syllogistic writing has to be learned because there simply isn't enough time to write great long essays debating each fact at length during exams and graders are looking for particular ideas in the essays. They aren't going to spend a great deal of time wading through murky waters of incorrectly formatted writing to ascertain whether or not you got the idea and whether you applied correct logic in coming to your conclusion. You need to put forth a major premise a minor premise and a conclusion. The issue and rule are the major ideas that you are going to present first. In order to do that correctly you have to have your issue spotting and definitions down pat. Then you get to the analysis after pulling the facts. The point between the major premise and the minor premise is where you shine.

For example:

Murder (major premise or issue)

Murder is the unlawful killing of another human being without justification or excuse. (major premise or rule)

Tommy killed Victor by stabbing him with a pitchfork over a farmland dispute. (facts that you pull from the pattern)

This is the ANALYSIS that comes from you. It's what ties the major premise to the fact This should be the bulk of you answer. Use quotes from the fact pattern and give valid reasons why Tommy is in your opinion able to be charged with first degree murder, depraved heart, manslaughter, etc.

Tommy committed murder (minor premise or conclusion)

The meat of your essay is going to be in the parsing of the elements and facts to support or deny they question that you asked first. The Bar is merely asking you to examine the issues and follow the threads in the fact pattern to a logical conclusion. A thorough written analysis will prove to them that you understand the issues hidden in the fact pattern and that you can present appropriate legal inferences based on those issues.

The test does not focus on rote memorization; its primary focus is to test your higher order thinking. The bulk of the grading is done in the analysis portion because showing that you can logically resolve the issues presented in a fact pattern is a critical part of practicing law. The law is not passive; it requires the active detection of issues and the careful application of laws and theories to successfully resolve the question.

You don't have to settle the questions at hand, just argue the question in a firm way. Show that you know more than the rule of law, show that you can successfully argue the points that the law turns on. Any analysis should be no less than a paragraph.

Good writing is concise but it will certainly carry your point. Overwriting is not necessary and in fact it wastes precious minutes. There is an art to condensing the monotonous minutiae that many attorneys envelope their writing in so that has the potential to be easily understood by a reader. That last sentence was not a good example.

The essays are an hour each and you don't have the time to write long winded sentences nor do the graders have the time to dissect them for meaning. Short, simple sentences are gold in your essay.

Don't insert your emotions into your analysis. Reasoning is, by its very nature, cool and detached. Even if a particular set of facts makes you feel emotional make sure you stay on the facts and reasoning. Ignore any urge to insert emotive writing or humor into the writing. The issues that your future clients present to you will rarely be rational or presented unemotionally. It's your job to shrug off bias and insert rationality and parity, to see the issue crystal clear and craft a winning argument. The essays test your ability to see issues even when clouded by the actions and feelings of the parties.

You have to analyze, think, write, and revise as you go. Usually those skills are very separate and it can be difficult to combine these tasks into a one hour essay. Many people struggle with writing and say "I'm no good at writing" simply because they aren't pushing out polished essays by the hour. Learning how to revise and write while in 1L is one of the most important tasks that your professors will teach you. Pay attention. I don't recommend laptops or tablets during class the first year because there is too much temptation to surf the web at the expense of listening to your professors. If you want to type your notes make sure you don't get online. Professors are coming into the room prepared and ready to teach and it's disrespectful to give them anything but 100% of your attention.

ESSAY STUDY TIPS

Rewriting the model answers can give you a leg up. Analyzing winning answers, deconstructing them, and rewriting them in your own words can quickly teach you to get a feel of what sounds and feels right when writing your own essays under timed conditions. There are also terms of art that you will learn to use as a matter of habit.

Take your time and figure out what makes the essay a "model" answer. Look at the sentence construction. Does it balance legal theory with individual analysis? Remember, these answers aren't perfect. No answer written in one hour is going to be, but they hold several things in common. Most of them flow; they have a good format with liberal use of bolding, underlining and spacing. The essays all follow the standard IRAC format.

The model answers state facts and then support the facts with evidence gleaned from the question. They don't make many assumptions and they are concise. The thoughts are arranged in a progressive, coherent, linear method. After reading the questions and rewriting the model answer think about what could have been added or deleted. What issues would you have expanded on, what would you have done better?

ESSAY EXERCISE I

The first exercise is pretty simple. Just loosen up your fingers and practice stream of consciousness writing. Stream of consciousness writing is usually a narrative device but it actually works well to develop the skill to keep your sentences flowing for an extended period of time. Pick out an issue in a fact pattern that you are reading, such as battery, negligence, or whatever else you see and begin writing. Write everything that comes to mind on that subject even if you add a lot of filler and things that are not quite right.

Write without pausing for ten minutes don't worry about spelling or grammar. The point of this exercise is to get your thoughts out of your head and onto the page as quickly as possible. The first few times you do this it's going to look strange and it's going to feel even stranger. Sentences are going to be garbled and there will be quite a bit of filler that you wouldn't dream of putting in a real essay. Do this regularly with all of the issues. Your writing skills and the way you access the buzz words for each issue will improve dramatically.

The reason for this exercise is so you can get those 1200+ words on paper when it comes down to the FYLSX. The last thing you need is to get stuck staring at a blinking cursor for 10 minutes while you gather your thoughts and try to generate sentences. An essay that is only an hour long and entails reading, editing, and analysis requires that you hit the ground running with minimal hesitation. Don't bother fixing spelling errors during this practice, that's what spell-check is for. Just WRITE!

ESSAY EXERCISE II

If you go through all your professors essays and the Bar essays then practice making your own. Shoot for hiding 7-12 issues in your essay. Learning how to write an essay is a huge step in learning how to deconstruct an essay. If you can put your own buzzwords in and see how it works then you will be able to recognize those same issues in other essays that you are presented with. Below is a sample essay that I wrote to practice hiding issues.

Question 1

Vanessa is a vocal anti-war and anti- homosexual critic and she goes with her church of fourteen members to various public events to promote their beliefs. Six of the members of the church are her immediate family. She has gone to protest with the entire congregation of her church at a local cemetery while the funeral of a popular local woman named Emma is going on. They spent the night before painting signs that had different messages on them. Some of the messages said that Emma was an evil woman because she supported veterans, homosexuals, and abortion. Some of the signs said that Emma was going to hell. They have remained on the public sidewalk adjoining the cemetery but Emma's family can still see them. Bob and Tina are the children of the Emma, who are neither gay nor anti-war. Her former husband Bo is present as well though he is not bothered by the protesters. After the ceremony several of Emma's family were enraged and charged at the protesters. The protesters yelled back waved anti-war posters at them and cursed Bob and Tina. Tina lashed out and waved her arms into Vanessa, the nearest protester. Bo walked up and pulled Tina away but he was hit by a poster waved by Vanessa in the middle of the issue.

CHAPTER 7: PREPARING YOUR MEMORY: LEARN ANYTHING QUICKLY

Your memory is the hardest worker in your head. It is your file cabinet, computer, and preparer, that will get you through the test. Without memory, long or short term, YOU as you and others know you would not exist. Figuring out how your memory works and honing its properties is how you learn more information with less time and effort. Your previous education probably hasn't prepared you for the volume of material that you wade through during the next few years.

If you don't get your memory in shape then it won't hold everything in. It's got to be the bodybuilder in your brain. Your memory will carry and support the load.

Don't confuse memorization with actual grasp of the material. You can't memorize everything and pass. It doesn't work that way because you need to get your logic centers in top shape too. Create a databank of memory based information and couple it with the understanding that active study gives. What does it matter to you if you have finally memorized all of the definitions but you don't know how to apply logic to them?

Books on memory techniques are valuable resources and many of them have interesting ways will to help you learn new ways of absorbing information. When you are learning a great deal of material quickly it is important to link the things you don't know to things that you DO know. Pictures associated with topics will keep them accessible in your head.

Silly pictures and scenes are easy to remember. For example, I learned *"Martin v. Reynolds"* for environmental trespass. by picturing a sheet of Reynolds aluminum foil walking into the apartment set of an older TV show called "Martin." Martin's neighbors were always sauntering into his apartment uninvited so it stuck out as a trespassing case. That made *"Martin v Reynolds"* come alive and I managed to do that with dozens of cases with no problem. It sounds cumbersome but it's not. This memorization technique is called the method of Loci and it works. Attaching words to pictures or scenes is perfect for remembering chunks of information.

Spend five minutes imagining a crazy scene. Think "Alice in Wonderland" wild. The farther from reality the scene is the easier it will stand out as a unique memory. You then hang your ideas onto each interesting part of the scene.

For defenses to contracts- first I imagined walking into a spacious gray room- I encountered a huge green frog ("Fraud" sounds like frog so it stuck). I looked around and saw a figure called "Duress" in a big yellow dress holding a gun to the frog's head. Further in "Illegality" was represented as a set of steel jail bars. Behind these imposing bars a massive steak sat cooling on a platter, "Mistake". Next on the platter was a concha pastry representing "Unconscionability." "Statute of Frauds" a group of 6 frogs as a stone fountain spouting water streams into the air (6 for the other MYLEGS mnemonic that you learn for that idea.)

This amount of detail sounds complicated but I learned the entire set of these defenses in 10 minutes while walking to the market one sunny day and just reinforced it for 3 or so minutes per day until it was ingrained. It was on a trip up North so I didn't even have access to all of my study materials. The ingraining process took a week and to booster it I closed my eyes and went through the scene once in a while. I can close my eyes and walk through the imagery now even if I haven't looked at it for six months because it's a memory now. Humans remember tangible items better than abstract words, even if those tangible items are imaginary.

Build as many of these "memory palaces" as you need. You won't run out of space because your brain has the capability. You can use rooms that you already know if you aren't in the mood to create a new elaborate scenario. I used my bedroom and mentally attached concepts to the things that live in my room. The lamp represented an element in a problem, the TV., as did the bookshelf, bed, and door among other things. When you absorb the information there's no longer a need to picture the room. It springs forth naturally.

Short Term Memory Storage

Many students study for hours and hours and don't feel like they are getting anywhere. This is probably because they are spending a lot of time and energy but getting the information stored in their short term memory. When they wish to retrieve it days or months later it's imperfectly stored or forgotten completely.

Tie your memories to things that you already know so it won't erode. Using the method of Loci and any other memory devices that you find useful cements the information so that once learned it's accessible with just a little bit of occasional reinforcement.

Long Term Memory Storage

When you make the effort to store the information in your long term memory it builds a foundation of that information that you can build upon instead of spending time re learning the same things over and over again. You can add a whole new level of theory and in depth knowledge once you can retrieve the material at will.

CHAPTER 8: MENTAL STRATEGY

A major part of any standardized exam is how you feel and react on exam day. A dramatic increase in stress stimuli is overwhelming for most people. This may only be a one day test. But imagine being on a roller coaster for eight straight hours with a one hour break. Stressful, huh?

Your should expect to be successful. To do that you have to have confidence and your anxiety levels need to be low. The atmosphere at the Convention Center is intense and you will probably run into some classmates milling around before the exam. People are pacing like caged animals before the doors open. Don't get caught up in the anxiety because the aura of the moment is anxiety producing. The security process is tight and the energy in the air is one of tension, excitement, and fear. The better prepared you go in there, the more confident you will feel.

There are methods to incorporate to settle these nerves. They should be worked on before test day because centering yourself during study improves retention and focus. Besides, you certainly don't want to miss out on passing due to panic or test anxiety. First, figure out your goals.

WRITE DOWN YOUR GOALS

You need to know where you're headed and how you're going to get there. Getting into law school is an achievement that should make you feel proud. However, that's just the beginning and you need goal posts to see you through.

Write down your academic objectives. If "pass the FYLSX on the first try" is an important metric of your success then write it down. But, you must also write down the micro goals that will get you to that point. Sample goals could be: Maintain a 2 hour per day study regimin: Be in the top 20% of your class: Limit personal engagements to two per month: Meditate five minutes per day on success. There are many small steps to take before you reach a big goal. Count those steps.

WRITE DOWN YOUR WEAKNESSES

I read once that students have better success rates if they write about their anxieties the night before a test. That resonates with me and spending a few minutes a day journaling about your fears sounds like a good use of time. Start a week before the test. Before you go to sleep the night before the test do it again. Journal about any personal issues that you feel may hold you back. Some people have panic issues. Some people have issues that would make them susceptible to self-sabotage. Some people freeze. If you are worried about being prepared, write that down. Get to know your soft spots so that these issues cannot interfere because you know them consciously. Usually the things that bubble up during high stress times are problems that we keep buried in our unconscious. There's a reason why Aristotle's great axiom was "Knowing yourself is the beginning of all wisdom."

This act isn't meant to amplify your test anxiety. It reduces these fears because you have spent time addressing them and seeing them nakedly. Once you have seen exactly what plagues you then there is no reason to let that voice speak to you during the test. It lays your self-doubt to rest (temporarily of course, look for it to blossom anew next semester.)

Take time to write about how you will feel if you fail. Write this because you need to understand the stakes. Failing isn't going to kill you. It may make you stronger, but it's important that you pass. Your GOAL is to pass. Failure is always a possibility but you cannot let its potential be a hindrance. You can always take the test again if you need to. But don't use that as an excuse.

ACKNOWLEDGE YOURSELF COMPLETELY

Don't harp on your weaknesses, work on them. Be honest with about what you and others have addressed in your study and writing habits. If you see deficits then work on them! Have a good attitude about fixing habits that can slow down your progress. Ask your professors for feedback their purpose is to get you through the first year and pass the FYLSX so their unbiased feedback helps a lot.

Conversely, list your strengths and feel good about the work that you have done. Confidence comes from recognizing all of the talents and skills that you posess. When you work hard you reap the rewards. So list out all of your strengths and keep working at them to get even better.

MEDITATE

If you are in any way spiritual now is the time to engage. If not, find some meditative practices to work with because clearing your head is a major step towards improving your ability to learn effectively and retain knowledge. If you are grounded and centered without a million things buzzing around in your head when you study then you are in a better position to sit down and work in a disciplined way.

Preparation begets confidence. Fill up those notebooks. You will end up with a stack of over a dozen, filled up writing on both sides of the page. These notebooks contain every definition written dozens of times, every legal explanation that you've hears, developed mnemonics, notes from the classes that you attend, and any other bits of information that you've accumulated over the school year. Seeing all that is a huge confidence boost.

The best way to begin is to understand exactly what the Bar wants from you at every stage of the test. If you spend time preparing yourself for every aspect then you will feel confident and relaxed on test day because you will be prepared and there will be no unexpected surprises. This should reduce some of the anxiety, if you know what's expected then you aren't venturing upstream without a paddle. You can make a game plan that will give you the maximum chance for success.

2-3 MONTHS BEFORE THE TEST

Some non ABA students haven't taken the LSAT because they opted not to compete for an ABA seat and some non ABA schools do not require it to gain admission. There are students who haven't taken a standardized exam in a long time. If tests give you any sort of anxiety, or if it's been many years since you have experienced a proctored test in a formal environment then take one before the FYLSX. Doing this will take some of the fear of the unknown out of the process and should put you more at ease. Getting familiar with a formal test environment will give you a level of control that home or school proctored tests just can't match. You don't want to go into an expensive career based test without having all the advantages that you can muster.

This is a 700+ dollar test that you only have a couple of attempts at if you want to proceed through 2L. Preparation is the cornerstone to success and one of the best ways to prepare is to simulate those experiences that will closely approximate the actual test experience. If you have any sort of test anxiety or you haven't taken a stone cold standardized test in a while then you should familiarize yourself by taking another test beforehand. Results don't matter for the practice test so take something that you don't have to study for.

 The point of this exercise is the experience. Sign up for a cheap Mensa exam ($40), a CLEP ($120 or so), the LSAT ($145) or another standardized exam that you can take close to the date of the FYLSX (a month or two beforehand). The stress level and formality of most of those tests are on par with the Baby Bar.

A lot of very capable, smart people have a big problem with taking standardized tests. Nerves, performance anxiety, and panic are just a few issues that people have. Taking a standardized test is a lot like giving a speech in a large hall. Some people have physical and emotional reactions to it. The best way to counteract the fear is to acclimate yourself to the stress and using relaxation practices. If that's the case for you then work on that and get used to the procedures before taking the exam. There's too much riding on this test to walk in cold.

TEST DAY

. Show up with comfortable and visually appropriate attire. Dress for comfort but don't wear your pajamas or ratty sweats. Look how you feel; relaxed, comfortable, and confident.

- Make sure that you have tested your exam software as the Bar requires.

- Fully charge your laptop, bring the cord for it and make sure that it is in good working order.

- Read the instructions that the Bar sends and adhere to every single rule.

Some people wear earplugs during the test and that's fine as long as you stay extremely cognizant of the time. The danger with earplugs is that you might not hear the proctors call the times before the test is over. If you decide to wear earplugs you should still to vary your levels of distraction when you study during the months before the test so that there are no unexpected surprises on game day. You can always adjust and take them off without being alarmed or distracted by the increase in noise.

DON'T FORGET YOUR LEARNING STYLE DURING THE EXAM:

Auditory learners-

Mouth the passages silently but "hear" them in your head. Close your eyes for a moment and inwardly dictate the analysis in your head for a moment when you get stuck, then get writing.

During lunch break go outside and give yourself an out loud pep talk. Talk to people around you but don't let any of their worry or stress rub off on you.

Kinetic Learners-

Remember to lift your arms and stretch every 10-20 minutes and write on your scratch paper when needed, cross your legs and move a bit when you need to (unobtrusive movements that will refocus you when needed)

During the break take a few minutes and walk up and down or around the block.

Visual Learners-

Close your eyes for a second and "see" your mnemonic situations. Quickly draw diagrams when you need to. Underline important sections on your essay and in your MCQ question booklet.

Write all over your scratch paper. Don't forget to bring plenty of extra pencils so that you can keep your pencil moving over your scratch paper and booklets.

CASES

I see a lot of value in learning an applicable case for each scenario. It doesn't take too much time once you start using your memorization techniques and it will give you a deeper understanding of 'why' certain laws are structured the way they are. The thing that makes this tricky is that you CANNOT get the case name or facts wrong if you are working it into your essay. You have to know each one flawlessly.

Rule 1: You will read hundreds of cases the first year and brief dozens.

Rule 2: You will promptly forget most of them.

Rule 3: The graders know this and it shows a special level of dedication if you can cite applicable cases or formulas when writing your essays.

The Learned Hand formula is useful for a lot of negligence discussions. Know the difference between the insanity tests; M'Naughten, American Law Institute (A.L.I.),

If you write Palsgraf v LIRR (1928) remember to put both Cardozo's majority opinion and Andrew's minority opinion, Hawkins v. McGee (1929), Martin v. Reynolds,

In a sea of essays yours will stand out and you are that much more likely to get into that golden 20%.

Summers v. Tice (1948).

United States v. Carroll Towing Co. (1947) (the "Hand Formula")

Bonus tips to get those extra points

Think of the points like Super Mario coins. You've got to work hard to get the maximum, running in a straight line won't get you as many as taking the time to jump around and go that extra mile. Learn a few case names for each subject and write about them in your analysis. Even if you are just going to discuss the case tangentially and then dismiss it as not entirely applicable it will still show that you are familiar with concepts and that you are able to analyze the subject in its entirety and dismiss points that will not bolster your case.

Rushing through each question and then grading 100 at a time will not give you the necessary experience to run through these questions later. Then grade those ten questions and the most important step...

get out your notebook or laptop (I usually prefer to handwrite as it takes a lot longer to write and that helps sink in the information and trains muscle memory faster.) I will write out the entire analysis, except for the obviously incorrect answers and really try to flesh out WHY a question was right or wrong. If you find something that you found a little difficult to understand re-read the question and then re write the correct answer until you understand the reasons why.

Conclusion

Hopefully you learned a lot of new information that will jump start your academic career. You now have the tools to succeed in law school and on your upcoming professional exams.